Fantasy
Life

Also by Mario Milosevic

Novels
Claypot Dreamstance
The Coma Monologues
The Doctor and the Clown
Kyle's War
The Last Giant
Splitting
Terrastina and Mazolli

Collections
15 Strange Tales of Crime and Mystery
Entangled Realities (with Kim Antieau)
Labor Days
Miniatures

Poetry
Animal Life
Love Life

Fantasy Life

poems by Mario Milosevic

 Green Snake
PUBLISHING

Fantasy Life
by Mario Milosevic

Copyright © 2004 by Mario Milosevic

ISBN-13 978-1-949644-14-2

No part of this book may be reproduced without written permission of the author.

Published by Green Snake Publishing
www.greensnakepublishing.com

for Kim

Contents

- 11 In the Hall of Records
- 12 Where Did All the Porches Go
- 13 Materialists Write the Best Ghost Stories
- 14 The Cloak of Death
- 16 The Circularity of Time
- 17 Out of Body Experience
- 18 Finding a Piece of the Day
- 19 The Secret Life of Telephones
- 20 Super Hero Takes the Month Off
- 21 The Last Melody
- 22 Curbside Wise Man
- 23 Migrations
- 24 Unlikely to Happen Any Time Soon
- 25 Before the Filter
- 26 Cartography
- 27 Time's Apologist
- 28 Like Pegasus After the Accident
- 29 Phantom Limbs
- 30 What if Words Had Guardian Angels
- 31 After Market
- 32 Doll, Still Living
- 34 Vistas
- 35 A Troublesome Vision of Apocalyptic Tendencies
- 36 A Vision

38   A Dismissive Adornment

39   Things Happen at the Library that Most People Know...

40   We Are All Ghosts

41   Browsing the Architecture Shelf at the Bookstore

42   Thoughts While Contemplating an Archaeological Dig

43   Power

44   The Great Divide

45   Atlas

46   A Field Guide to the Phosphenes

48   House Keys Are Dedicated Monogamists

49   Inventory

50   The Past

52   Twelve Things a Man Should Do After Dying

53   A Kind of Grief

54   Lunar Fate

55   Benign Encounter

56   Wondering What They Are Up to in the Middle of the Night

57   A Trail of Meanings

58   Settled on the Sky

59   The 4th Little Pig

60   Faded Hues

61   Reincarnation

62   The Places We Have Exceeded

63 When I Die
64 The World is a Strange Place
65 The Real Scoop About Pixies
66 The Ghost of Ghost
67 Magician
68 Upon a Star
69 The Man Who Ate Everything
70 The Unexpected Unexplained
71 The Gift of the Sea
72 Ghosts
73 Do Not Step on the Top Rung
74 My Bicycle
75 Legends
76 A Fable
77 The Ultimate Truth
78 Western Civilization
79 Some Kind of Joke
80 What People Care About
82 The Wake
83 Galapagos
84 While Considering the Possibility of Using the Columbia...
85 Origami Landscape
86 Out of the Park
88 My Encounter With the Oracle

89 After Dreams Have Scattered
90 Fair Use
91 Jason and the Argonauts
92 The Camouflage of Fantasy
93 He's the Same Age as I Am
94 Never the Moon
96 Strange Things Can Happen on the Path Next to Falls Creek
97 Mark

100 Dramatis Personae
102 Acknowledgements
104 About the Author

In the Hall of Records

My odyssey through the hall of records
began with a sad encounter at the entrance.

The keeper at the gate saw my rags and
knew I was unable to pay the admittance fee.

He pulled rumpled paper money from his own
pocket and put it in the barrel and looked

at me with a kind of empty stare. He knew.
Inside the hall I found corridors criss-

crossing a vast chamber with ceilings
higher than the sky. The floor at my feet

was transparent and I could look down and
see more corridors on the floors beneath

me and everywhere people walking, people
running, some sobbing, and only a few of

them happy. Everything was written down
here, I had been told in the stories that

we heard from the time we were children.
Everything, every moment, every second.

In the hall of records I could find the
time to pursue the meaning of my life.

In the hall of records I put my head down
on the glass floor and I floated to sleep.

Where Did All the Porches Go

I'm guessing fairies
came in the night
somewhere about the mid
to late sixties
and erased them
from all the house plans.
They probably thought
we didn't appreciate
these little incursions
into their realm,
and contractors are
not noted for defying
the magical folk.
Part house part yard,
porches were the twilight
portions of human houses.
They existed between worlds.
If you spent time in one
you'd never want to leave,
and fairies are stubborn.
They like their space.

Materialists Write the Best Ghost Stories

because it scares them to think
they might be wrong
when they say reality
is a physical construct
unmarred by the vapors
of illusion that would corrode
the solidity of a life lived
by the rules of matter
not the whims of mind
that create the sleek
easy musings that come with
those smoky apparitions
curling up out of nothing
and crawling into your heart
stopping you with the beat
of a life unseen
there inside you holding on
soft iron grip
and old age of pulsing
quickening cold blood
projected like slow glass
dimming fading quiet

The Cloak of Death

Death left his cloak on a hook
by the front door. I hesitated
when I saw it, then took

it and ran after Death, who had sped
on his way, apparently pleased
to have completely and finally shed

himself of what must once have seized
his imagination with attractive morbid thoughts.
I never caught up with Death. He breezed

out of my life. Did he have the hots
for some raven-haired beauty unknown
to us mortals? Or was it lots

of loafing time, away from phone
and fax that made him abdicate
his long held troublesome throne?

Ah, well. His motives of late
have seemed arbitrary and odd
anyway. Perhaps he's become irate

at having to maintain a facade
of calm calculating efficiency.
But now here I am with Death's shod

hood and cape, a length of spun ebony,
the crisp uniform of the most
famous harvester in history.

Part of me wants to show it off, boast
to my friends about how Death left
his clothes and ran off to the coast.

But its dry scratchy peculiar heft
convinces me to cut it into squares
and give it to a quilt maker who's bereft

of material for her craft. She prepares
a patchwork blanket with the pieces
and I sleep under it, murmuring happy prayers.

The Circularity of Time

The Supreme Fascist
has déjà vu.
I have an odd feeling,
he mutters,
like I've created
this universe before.
It's as though I know
exactly what horrible fate
is going to befall
all of these creatures
because it has all happened
exactly this way before.
He sits with the oddness
until it passes.
Then he laughs.
That was really weird,
he says, and returns to work
concocting plagues
and natural disasters
for his supreme amusement
while his people
groan and whisper
not again not again not again.

Out of Body Experience

in hospitals they know
that people who die
during operations
and come back
frequently report
leaving their bodies and
floating near the ceiling
where they watch
the surgeons and nurses at work
hear them talk about the weather
see their own bodies
shrouded in clean white
a red wound affording access
to their heart or liver or lungs
scrambling their perceptions
to such an extent
that many rational types
simply don't believe them
and medical institutions have taken
to placing messages
on the tops of cabinets so that
when a patient recovers
and says
Doc I flew
the attending physician
can ignore the wonder of it
and try to verify the claim
by inquiring as to what exactly
the o.r. aviator observed
on the top shelf of the
operating room garment rack
as though
a free floating soul
had nothing better to do
than participate
in an experiment designed
to prove the cleaving
and reuniting
of bone and being
never really happened
in the first place

Finding a Piece of the Day

Lightcicles dripped, melting from the
bright fruit atop the former tree.

A kind of daylight pooled at the base
like a little sun trying to scorch

the ground. We played hide and go
seek using that pole for home.

Raced "it" across grassy yards
in the early evening, each

of us trying to be the first to
touch the dry wood, pieces of

it split off in rough shards, the
winner of each race embraced,

covered in yellow light like all
the living bathed in streaming heat.

The Secret Life of Telephones

When we're not looking
they like to snicker
at us. Not in a nasty way,
just to have a little fun.

Sometimes, when they've
been on the hook for a while,
they miss the sound of a dial
tone and feel very sad.

Some telephones get tired
of carrying other people's
words and try to speak for
themselves. You might want

to think about your phone's
deepest desires the next
time you hear an annoying
blast of incoherent static.

Telephones know they are
connected in a vast community.
Many of them regard the busy
signal as a kind of heart beat.

Super Hero Takes the Month Off

The comic books
come back from the printer
with all the detailed
and sumptuous drawings
of Captain Supremo
replaced by crude
stick figures.
"I had vacation hours
accumulated," says
The Supe from behind
a margarita. "If I didn't
take 'em, I was gonna
lose 'em." Then he shrugs.
"What's the big deal?
We have replacements
on staff for a reason."
Stick Man quickly gains
a fan base. He fights
crime by slithering into
the drawings of the
criminals in the comic
books, then animating
their limbs into putting
down their weapons and
surrendering to authorities.
Captain Supremo finishes
his vacation but the comic
book editors don't let him
return to his previous life.
Stick Man watches him shuffle off.
Stick Man saves the world.

The Last Melody

Our graves compose a silent city,
the soft blocks gridding the ground.

Marble towers rise high to a measured
stillness and we cry for what once moved.

Above us the course of music is clear.
Below us a muffled mass holds blindness.

The curse of routine is our eternity now.
No refrain will open the caskets dreaming.

The parents will live in another city,
and hope undying does nothing here.

Dry throats scratch only parched tunes
and we know the old songs best of all.

The radio flies with remembered melodies.
My companions in the black yearn to raise

their old recumbent voices. A score may
always be entered in the record book.

We compose a layered symphony of our sleep:
a tune of mournful means and low hopes,

the air caressing soft paths only.
A callused trail of ancient treadings

leads quietly to this beatific mosaic.
And sing the songs that have made us sad.

Curbside Wise Man

He said: you think a ghost
is made of nothing?

Could nothing
have the muscle power

to haul around
a body all day?

Could nothing
scare the gee willickers

right of out of you?
Could nothing

live in a machine,
and most of all,

could nothing
make you want to drop

some change into my cup
to shut nothing up?

Migrations

Tiny spiders flowed from
the dry nib of my pen
and lined up on the page
in words describing a
blind woman's cane sniffing
the ground like a dog.

The gas station attendant
pumped blood into my tank
and gave me a pair of dice
with eyeballs in place of
the familiar black dots.
The eyes all blinked at
the same time, periodically
turning the dice into solid
cubes of pure white.

I drove past a herd of
cows knee deep in a field
without grass, wading
through the earth like
children pulling their
legs through blue pool water
trailing deep pink trenches.

And I was relieved to
see the mountain folding
itself up and moving into
a doll house next to
the limestone fireplace.

Unlikely to Happen Any Time Soon

I sometimes think about
what it would be like
to live on an ant's back.
I'd hold onto that
smooth hard shell,
vibrating like bones
in an earthquake
from her tiny heart,
and we'd crawl together
over juicy nasturtium buds.
If the colony sensed
some melted chocolate
several yards away
we'd be off for the good
of all, a road trip
over any terrain,
pushing on tirelessly
to retrieve that
precious sustenance.
The rest of the ants
would always be with us,
their collective mind
showing us the way.
My host's antennae would
wave confidently in front
of me, like twin batons
orchestrating the journey
of her life. She'd be
playing out the score
of a hundred million years
and I'd sleep, protected
by her delicate purrs.

Before the Filter

a big arugula taste of sunspots always
suggests an eleven year salad cycle

the green crud like turned cheese on
the hour glass wings of a luna moth

my glowing phosphene bulge tapping
the roof tar smell of a passing truck

they cotton to the fabric of reality
after tripping over a coil of kelp

the beach contains dusty chalk erasers
in a nascent ordered disturbance wave

and a clear smooth line of engagement
shows only a length of dental floss

where the blurry arc of a rainbow still
reaches past the water cycle flowchart

to find a tempera grain of truth lurking
in the sound of cumin touching a tongue

Cartography

He drew the most detailed map
he could, to scale, and fell
into it, a flat world threaded
with dry ink trails. He rose
on lines of elevation marks.
Had to find the top. The mountain
peak centered with numbers
indicating feet above sea level.
The steady going up. The longing
to see. The awful crisscross
of fibers pulling at his feet.

Time's Apologist

Last week
when I was 3 years old
and just learning about clocks
I thought I could count
how many times the second hand
would have to turn
before my life would be over.
I started at 1
watching the thin line of metal
sweep over the dial's face
then went to 2
and 3 and 4
before I got bored
with the exercise
and decided time
could get on very well
without my interference
in its odd need
to have each minute
follow another
in step wise succession.

Like Pegasus After the Accident

Shorn of wings made of dreams,
I push off the Earth with steps
measured by eternity's clock,
each footfall keeping me home.
Each spring-arched attempt at flight
crumbles to an aborted take off.

My back aches for the sinewy pull
of muscles rooted at my shoulder blades:
supporting feather pulses on a hinged lattice
of bone work. Holding my weight in a weightless
rising, memories soaring from a lost epoch
when air currents delineated my home.

And the miniature doll house landscapes,
now enveloping me, were just ports
for distant temporary moorings,
a shoreline holding fast
against the rush of wind tide
preserving a too-safe landing zone.

Phantom Limbs

Weeping willow
crying for your branches
broken off in a wind storm.
Do you still feel the buds
growing on the missing limbs?
Do you crave
the scratch of bird feet
scraping away
an irritating itch
still there where fibrous flesh
wrapped in bark skin
once hung from your trunk?
If I could
I would pick out
the ghostly tunneling bugs
tormenting you
with their
invisible chewing.

What if Words Had Guardian Angels

You'd hear them praying when you
pressed your ear to a printed page.
"Please keep me from the pain,"
you'd hear *death* say on its sighing
expelled breath, "of being deployed
in all those heart-breaking sentences."
Disease would likewise ask for absence
from so many bad news paragraphs.
"We can't take it anymore," says
cancer. "We can no longer summon
the strength we need to witness
the horrors we name," says *war* and
genocide, *killer* and *body count*.

Would they listen, these angels?
Would we suddenly see pages with
blank spaces where these agonized
words once dwelled? Would they get
words the help they needed from trained
professionals who could heal their
trauma? Or would the angels, invoking
the grim paradigm of the necessity of
facing even awful truths, simply bless
them with syllables of their own?
Offering their own sad words, would
they say: "You are *strong*. You will *live*.
You will see better days filled with *love*."

After Market

The shop had
some old used
months for sale.

There was a cute
September from
the 1950s, kind

of quiet, a little
fearful, maybe,
hiding in a corner.

The shopkeeper
tried to push a
May from 1824 onto

me but I resisted.
I guessed it had
been gathering dust

there this long for
a reason. Here's the
one for me, I said.

I reached behind a
pile of months from
the depression and

snagged a nice little
May from the late
1970s, the pioneering

years of nostalgia.
When everything
seemed better if it

was old and that way
of seeing the world
was still a bit new.

Doll, Still Living

In retirement, Barbie
spent her days
chain smoking unfiltered Camels
and watching soap operas.

She understood the characters
and their problems.
Honey, she'd say to the TV,
dump the dickless bastard.
You can do better.

Once, years after her
last public appearance,
she was called before
a congressional committee
to speak on the issue
of plastic surgery
being covered by Medicare.

I owe my career
and all that I am
to polymer technology,
she testified.

As she walked to
her limousine to leave
the Capitol some of her
local fans tried to push
past her bodyguards.

We love you, they shouted.
Retirement Barbie raised
her stiff arm and waved
her hand like a zombie.

Her fans bounced up
and down and screamed
like teenage girls at
a Beatles concert.

Barbie's limo driver
waited for her to
finish signing autographs;
then he handed her a tissue
which she used to wipe away
her imaginary Barbie tears.

Thanks Ken, she sniffled,
you glorious, hopeless,
fucked-up wonder.

Vistas

Could I have been a bird
in another life?
How else explain
my affinity for those
bird's eye views
of expansive landscapes?
They are like memories
of forgotten eras,
when the hairs on my arms
were feathers
and my toes were talons.
I'd catch the rising thermals,
wheel slowly over wide fields
and pity the creatures
plodding along,
looking up at me
and wondering:
What do we look like
form way up there?

A Troublesome Vision of Apocalyptic Tendencies

Broken clocks
and alien dreams
have come here
before their time.

We keepers collect
the chunks of life
that beach upon
our jagged shores.

But mute acceptance
puts a tailored
demand on more
than just the light.

And the chatter of
stars will move the
Earth when humans
have stepped aside.

Not done yet
the baking of the
world and all the
raisins in it.

An eternal rising
calls for endless
hope until the
groundswell quickens.

They come to us
we go to them
in mutual haste
and caution.

And then the rush
conveys our motion
and turns mere breath
to endless spirals.

A Vision

In the darkness a weary
old man lies sleeping,
his fingers tied with
pieces of string.
Their lengths trail
off the bed and
out the bedroom door.
Periodically the old man
shifts in his sleep, tugging
and jerking the strings.
As he does so people all
over the world accidentally
burn themselves
and say hurtful things
they did not mean to say
and have affairs they did
not want to have and
indulge in addictions
they thought they had
beaten. This goes on for
a long time. The old man
is very tired. He used
to be a master puppeteer, but
now that is all behind him
and he sleeps, oblivious to
what is happening in the world.

A group of heroes and heras,
ready to save the world,
enters the old man's room,
each carrying a pair of scissors.
They work a long time,
cutting the strings attached
to the old man's fingers.
They are quiet, careful not to
wake him. When they are done
they wordlessly slip away and
congratulate each other for
saving the world but when they
return they see nothing has changed.

People still act impulsively and destructively. Stunned, the would-be saviors sit silently, all their bravado and passion dissipated.

And the old man? He had the best night of sleep ever.

A Dismissive Adornment

The rendering in silver of
a child-eyed bug-faced alien

pinned to the purple lapel
of the county commissioner

at a legislative session to
debate the wisdom of enacting

a law protecting the creature
known as Bigfoot does not

wink or smile or show any
inclination to crack the

robot facade as smooth as a
legislator's glancing truth.

Things Happen at the Library that Most People Know Nothing About

The character containment officer
was sternly critical of our shoddy
practices. "You can't leave these
books open like this," she said.
"All the protagonists and villains,
even the cardboard characters,
will just leak out into the room.
Why do you think books are made
with covers? For looks?" Red-faced,
we closed all the books that had
been lying open, then corralled
the little creatures that had come
up out of the pages. They squirmed
in our hands and we tried to be gentle
but they did not want to go back.
A couple of us got tiny bites on our
fingers and palms. "How do they get
back into the books?" we asked the
containment officer. She held out
a bag and we dropped them into that
dark space. "It's at the stroke of
midnight when the gate opens up again,"
she said. "We'll have to move in
a grandfather clock that gongs with
the right sound and set it up so it
synchronizes with true midnight. We'll
take care of it. It's all part of the
service." We nodded sheepishly. Said it
would never happen again, we learned
our lesson. "I hope so," she said.
"Some libraries get overrun you know.
Sometimes they take over and
there's nothing anyone can do."

We Are All Ghosts

He said: We are all ghosts,
you and I and everyone.
But see how some of us
choose to haul bodies
around with us everywhere.

The stitches loosen over
time and we become
unmoored like oversized
balloons wary of errant
pinpricks. We are not
here to see the future.

Browsing the Architecture Shelf at the Bookstore

Volumes of them talking.
Of ancient cities and
how to build with straw bales.
Fit corner to corner.
See patterns. Raise the roof.
People live in these poems,
metered from stone and wood,
each floor rhyming the windows
above and below.
Bricks like blocky letter forms.
The words keeping back the rain.
Stanzas a storied epic holding up
the world with anti-gravity,
a lightness of purpose
and squeaky floor boards.
Sticky door like a metaphor
that won't quite click.

Thoughts While Contemplating An Archaeological Dig

Voices muted by weariness,
the stones speak now
mostly in the soft memory of million-year-old
brain structures amplifying the inner voice
that's congruent with granite's growl
and the harsh hot fury of genesis
in a cooling lava crust.
Before the green invasion
and the odd decoration of animated tissue,
there was only the hard reality
of dense structure,
conversing with simple grammars
made of cracks and scrapes.
It's a lost language in this era,
muffled by soil, roots, and leaves,
but preserved, perhaps,
in the song of pouring gravel
and the sharp ping
of a boulder cracking open,
its interior displayed
like a declarative sentence
delineating the story of the world.

Power

I wonder if Jerry Siegel
and Joe Shuster had ever
read Friedrich Nietzsche.
When their blue and red
clad übermensch lifted
that car over his head on
the cover of Action Comics,
was it an expression of "the
will to creative power,"
as the philosopher had
famously put it? Or did Joe
and Jerry just think it was
an image so appealing to
kids that it would induce
them to gladly part with
five cents for the privilege
of owning a copy, rather
than using those pennies
to buy something sensible
like bubble gum or licorice?

The Great Divide

Forget the white light beckoning
and the receiving line of your ancestors
with background music by an angel chorus.
Death isn't like that at all.
I've talked to ghosts
who've been through it
and they've told me:
How that white light
is an afterimage left over
on your retina. It disappears
in a few minutes and everything
is dark. And what about all your
relatives greeting you as you enter?
Nope. Just some generic figures
lining your pathway like Wal-Mart greeters
doing their jobs and nothing more.
Do I need to go on? The music:
whatever you happened to be listening to
at the moment of death.
Imagine a TV show theme
stretched out to infinity.
No wonder so many of them
want to come back to this world
and spend some quality time haunting us.
No wonder it takes a while
to get used to the way
they do things over there.

Atlas

The leaking ocean
dripped water
down the length
of his back.

He always in all ways
hated when that
happened. It was
getting late anyway.

If he could just
put it down
for a second
and look up.

See the world
at last. Hold the view
for a long time,
shouldered in his memory.

A Field Guide to the Phosphenes

Welcome to Eye
Theater. Today you
will be dazzled
by your own
retinal perceptions.
Begin your tour here.
Touch your eyeball
through your closed
eyelid. The point
opposite your finger
tip will sprout
a bubble of
light-rimmed darkness.
Press the heels
of your hands
to your eyes.
Your field of
vision will vibrate
with distorted black
and yellow checkerboard
patterns and pulsate
with blobs of
glowing light. A
caution to the
viewer: do not
perform eye theater
for too long.
A few seconds
is about right.
The pressure needed
to maintain the
spectacle can be
painful. Do tell
your friends about
what you saw.
No donation is
necessary. We have
no gift shop.

Feel free to
follow the vision
as far as
you wish it
to take you.
If you choose
not to return
we understand. We
will inform your
family of your
decision. Please confine
yourself to the
marked path and
enjoy your visit
to Eye Theater.

House Keys
Are Dedicated
Monogamists

They save
themselves
for only

one door.
Keys won't
mate with

strangers.
They adore
the warmth

of your
soft pocket.
Like happy

homebodies
they favor
kitchen

tables and
the tops
of dressers.

They never
take their
rings off.

Keys know
the power
of loyalty.

Inventory

Clouds in my pocket
like bits of lint.
Stars stuck between
my fingers sharp
as sand grains.
The globe a lone
marble damp and
rattling around
under the car seat.
Identity cruising
along with no where
to go. No way to
make it something
else.

The Past

According to some accounts of
reincarnation, returning souls
must eat a bowl of soup that
erases any memory of their
past lives before taking up their
new existence. This sounds like a
typically convoluted theological
construct designed to make an
attractive fairy tale fit into what
we take to be reality, but okay: let's
say it's true. You're sitting at a strange
table, after you've died, with a spoon
in your hand, and a big bowl of
chowder steaming in front of you.
You're supposed to dig in, but you
don't want to forget, not yet. You're
still savoring the memories of your
life. Why have them, if you can't
enjoy them? But the soup, see, it's
getting cold and you feel like you
probably shouldn't make trouble with
the people that control your re-entry
into the realm of the living. Maybe it's
within their power to cut you loose, let
you drift off into—what? That unknown
makes you uneasy. You look around.
Others are lapping up their soup like
there's no tomorrow to insure there
is a tomorrow, for them. By the time
they get to the bottom of their bowls,
a blank look has spread over their faces.
Already they're forgetting they had
spouses, children, careers, joys, frights,
tears. Soon they'll rise from the
table and get their new assignments,
their new lives. And it won't even
seem new, that's the thing, it'll seem
like the only thing they've ever
experienced. So all that came before

doesn't matter? You push the bowl
away from you. You think about that
time when you were a kid and you
climbed up that big oak tree in the
backyard and how when you got as
high as you could go, when the limbs
started getting too small to support
you, that's when you stopped to admire
the view. That's when you realized
the ground was miles below you, way
too far to risk climbing down from the
tree and you knew you were going to
be there a long time and you looked
around, fear catching in your dry throat,
adrenaline pulsing a thrilling rush
through your muscles. Your horizon
just moved a few miles and you knew
that if you ever came down from these
high leaves, your life would be
changed forever.

Twelve Things a Man Should Do After Dying

1. Refrain from haunting those you've left behind. It's not charming, it's tiresome.

2. Take up a hobby. You've got a lot of time on your hands now, fill it with something productive.

3. Don't complain about how some people get a better deal in the afterlife than you. Did you think inequality would magically disappear with death?

4. Rot quietly.

5. If you find yourself on a reincarnation track, accept with humility whatever creature is assigned to you. All have their place in the world, even slimy disgusting slugs.

6. Don't brag about the workmanship of your coffin. No one cares.

7. And while we're on the subject, don't keep bringing up how great your life was. No one cares about that either.

8. If you died by some disfiguring injury or disease, think about getting yourself fixed up. There are a lot of dead people and we all have to look at you.

9. Don't point out how cold it is. We all know it's cold. Every one of us.

10. Pay your dues on time.

11. Keep your religious affiliation to yourself. It's over. There's nothing to debate. Everyone knows who was right.

12. Smile. It really could be worse.

13. Bonus piece of advice: Steer clear of the newcomers until they've become acclimated. Most of them are pretty obnoxious at first.

A Kind of Grief

I joined the Tick Tock Club.
Every month they send me
a big parcel of time.
When I open it, everything—
the cat, the plants, the
decay, the blood, the dust—
it all moves as slowly
as smoke filling a sky.
The extra minutes stain
the house a striking blue
and visitors always remark
on how relaxed they feel.
My packages from the Tick
Tock Club always arrive
precisely on time. I could
set my clock by it. When
all the minutes go past
their expiration date I am
as sad as a little boy
whose puppy has just died.
I gather up the stale
minutes and clutch them
to me wanting them to
come back to life and
desperately numbly I
wish for that impossible
shade of blue to return.

Lunar Fate

I remembered when the moon will fall
quietly tracking across the sky
in its accustomed arc
then one tip of its crescent
snagging on a branch
of a hillside tree
and just like that
the inspiration for poets
and the engine of tides
will have been moored
on the horizon's edge
where it will sway in the breeze
like a great slow balloon
and children will gather round
with hands outstretched
to a clever entrepreneur
who will have secured the right
to cut up the moon into small pieces
and sell them for a dollar each
to the children who will mistake them
for candy at first
then collect and trade
pieces of the moon
like they were baseball cards
until one day all those pieces
will end up
in attics and the backs of closets,
forgotten artifacts of childhood

Benign Encounter

It plucked him
from the river
and tossed him
onto a small oasis
of grass and clover.
It watched as
he stood and shook
drops onto the
green cushion
supporting his soles.
He turned his head.
A landscape unknown
to him brushed
his eyes with
color and texture.
It moved away.
He reached for it
as it shrunk.
And never knew
its name.

Wondering What They Are Up to in the Middle of the Night

I guess I can accept the idea
that a fairy takes your baby teeth
and leaves you some coins
as fair trade.

But what I want to know
is what does she do with those teeth?

Does she make jewelry from them?
Macabre earrings, say, or lumpy necklaces
which she then sells at Saturday Market?

Or does she crush them
into a fine calcium powder
to help push away
the pixie version of osteoporosis?

Or maybe she fashions tiny dice
from all those canines and bicuspids
to use on casino night at the enchanted meadow.

This whole disturbing business
of trafficking in body parts,
well, it just troubles me a little,
thinking how the young
are made unwitting partners
to strange practices
they are not equipped to understand.

A Trail of Meanings

I dip my pen into the night
draw up the darkness there
spill it onto the bright page
like a trail of thick blood.

A few stars stud the line
like gritty bits of sand
that get under your fingernails
when you harvest potatoes.

I think to brush away
those tiny fires
hot like microscopic stoves
then hold my hands over them.

Their heat toasts my words
and warms my palms
while I balance the pen
between my fingers and wait.

Settled on the Sky

Settled on the sky,
I built my house
expansively to bring
those spaces close.

The beanstalk ceilings
where giants lived
explained the ways
of birds for me.

With a rapid heart
beating and a face
tinged red I stretched
my self on the floor.

And looked up to
a wind constructing
worlds strung between
the wooden beams.

The tiles pressing
on my back melted
like warm jelly.
I gulped quietly,

grabbed for some
thing I could not
see in the pillars
of air holding me up.

The 4th Little Pig

Not straw or wood or
stone. The forgotten

pig chose fire and
lived fat and happy

in another world
behind walls made

of flame. Even the
wolf turned from

this house to look
elsewhere. The smoke

was like cottony fog
moving over a brain.

It obscured the view
and erased everything:

landscape, sight, fear,
memory, love, and hope.

Faded Hues

An awkward glance
across an eon;
looking for the parcel of time
where I used to grow
and where I can find
the colors I need
to tint the world.

I carry a brush
and dip it into the past;
raise its saturated tip,
and sweep it dripping
across the years
to the present
where its load
flows onto the life
around me.

I greet the image
of my greener self,
all wet and newly formed,
with welcoming words
to quell the terror living
in his heart
and crawling up to his eyes.

Reincarnation

Maybe I was someone else
in another life. Or maybe I
didn't want to bother with
a new identity and just came
back as myself. Or maybe I
let the fates roll the dice and
went along with whatever
turned up. Or maybe I forgot
everything and I've been
through here many times
in the past and don't remember
any of it. I could be the kind
of soul that just doesn't know
its own place in the shuffle.
Maybe no one else has ever
come back except me. Maybe
everyone comes back except
me. Maybe the past is really
the future, and my dreams are
memories of events to come.
Some of them, anyway. Maybe
Halloween with its masks and
costumes is a re-enactment of
the process and that's why once
a year we are charmed by disguised
children looking for debased
nourishment at our doors.
Maybe they remind us of cloaked
souls seeking sustenance and
re-entry through the portal
back into the warm light.

The Places We Have Exceeded

She has seen one city. But also
infinite variations of the city.

Every day she enters her life anew.
It's all here:

Fingerprints, swaying motion, toothbrush,
scars, tea cups, voices, the need to see.

All the words won't fit into her head
and all the tales come from somewhere else.

Creation myths open her world to death.
Why have stories always been necessary?

How do the delicate structures conspire
to lift her face to the constellations?

The ink is red like the blood of a cut.
A rose concentrates the life of love.

Where will the end be when the stories stop?
Only the heat of suns can silence hope.

Tales have been wrapped around her life
in the same way green hugs a flower stem.

Spiral hopes enter a moon's serrated shadow.
The final turning grips like ghost love.

When I Die

Don't burn me to ash.
I want to be food
for worms and bugs.
They should gobble up
all the bits of me
and when they later
get together for their
squishy little reunions,
I'll be there: the itch
at their collective ear.
I'll say: remember me,
that great meal you
had a few weeks ago?
I will be the voice
in their group mind.
Like a ghost creeping,
I'll be right behind them,
haunting their tiny lives
and seeing the ground
through small eyes
never blinking.

The World is a Strange Place

I found out where the things I forget go to.
It was on the internet.
How the memories no one wants anymore
fly around in the air for a while,
then end up at an underground storage facility
in the remote desert in northern Nevada.
The memories get buried
in the geologically stable rocks there,
and once they are deposited
it's all over.
You can never get them back.
Some people actually go there
in a kind of pilgrimage
to release their memories.
A retired librarian runs the place
and takes good care of the memories,
being careful not to catalog any of them,
but happy to show off
some of the more interesting ones.
The painful ones get looked at a lot.
They're the ones people don't want to own or carry.
The ones that hurt too much.
The ones they wish they never had.

The Real Scoop About Pixies

The fairies are not polite beings.
Most people don't know this,
but when they want some of your hair
or bits of your fingernails, they don't wait
for you to trim them from your body.
No, they come right into the house
and without so much as a hello
or an excuse me please, they set to work
pulling off what they want
for their spells and such.
I wouldn't mind so much except
they also don't pay much attention
to the amount of pain they inflict
during their removal operations.
They'll yank at your eyebrows
(they really like those hairs,
no one knows why) like they are
gold ingots and kick you
in the eyeball if you dare to
question their motives or their methods.
If they have any kind of sharp implement
it is invariably in poor maintenance,
rusty and dull, never up to the job at hand.
On top of it all, none of them
ever says thank you or leaves
any kind of gift or offering.
But if you should ever forget
to put out a plate for them,
my, my, the fuss that ensues
is not to be witnessed by those
at all offended by harsh language.
If you want to know the truth
I don't even think they are all that cute.
Or sprightly. Freeloaders, every one
of them, living on the world's good graces
because we think they live an enchanted life.
About as enchanting as rats, if you ask me.
Me, with shorn brows, and fingernails pared
to the quick. Me, wondering if maybe,
just maybe, they are punishment for some
transgression I've long since forgotten.

The Ghost of Ghost

Life selects the cautious ones for long life.
That bright-eyed stray cat we named Ghost was born
a reckless soul. Friendly with everyone,

and a fierce hunter, unafraid to dash
into traffic or prowl through blackberry
vines if he sensed a scurrying meal there.

His grand vaporous presence disappeared
periodically. Out catting around
no doubt, for such behavior must have been

part of his own genesis. But those eyes
were clouded over like milky marbles
that day we found him stiff at pavement's edge.

Death was his hard reprimand but his death,
even long months after we buried him,
did not keep him from being. Here with us.

Magician

A card picked me and guessed who
I was. Later it changed me into
a diamond. This fooled everyone
in the audience who expected a
club. The doves and rabbits became
allies. They lived in a world
of silk scarves and enjoyed
disappearing and reappearing
for days on end. The flowers
and coins had their own culture.
They breathed a different air.

Upon a Star

If the stars
should all fall

out of the sky
this cold night

and collect
on the ground

like heaps
of bright rice

left after
the wedding guests

have departed,
then who

are all the
wishes for?

The Man Who Ate Everything

Started out with his backyard,
an appetizer. Several courses
of continents and oceans followed.
It was not enough. The entire
planet, swallowed whole.
The moon next. More feasting.
It was a frenzy. Asteroids like
candies, the sun like the
hottest of peppers. Insatiable,
now, the eating became all
consuming: star clusters that
hung together like peanuts
in chocolate. Interstellar dust
served up like whipped cream.
Could there be room for more?
Galaxies chewed up and swallowed.
Great gobs of them in the man's
belly, a universe there, the
edges of it like the sweetest
of pie crusts: more delicate
than insect wings, tapering
into emptiness.

The Unexpected Unexplained

The ghosts were complaining again
last night. They don't like that
they're sinking into the ground.
No one told them it would be like
this. They want to be haunting the
living and taking effortless trips
through the air, floating like dreams
of flying. That was the promise.

But now they cry and they moan
and their sounds come up and fill
the world for as long as they can
before the grains of dirt and the
dense rock muffles whatever stories
they still have in them. Leftovers
trying to nourish the spirits of
you and me.

The Gift of the Sea

Don't think I understand
the moans of the Earth
any better than you do.
If the planet suddenly
swept the dinner table
clear of dishes, cutlery,
and napkins, and its
hunger pains exploded into
writhing hurting voice,
would you know how
to interpret the sound?
Would you know how to answer?
I think I would take a
great kelp from the ocean
and flop it down
on the table and garnish it
with a froth of white bubbles
and say to the Earth:
"This seaweed and this foam
came from your sister, the sea."
I don't know what
would happen next but
in my inner eye I
see the Earth take a
breath and with my inner
ear I hear the Earth
sigh and invoking my inner
voice I explain that all
the broken crockery and
the clatter of silver will
take care of itself
and with my
inner heart I offer
thanks for the peace
of a meal consumed
in warm harmony
and earth-water yin-yang.

Ghosts

are opportunists.
They attach themselves
to fresh corpses,
drinking up all that's there
in the expiring flesh,
then humming along on it
like newly fueled automobiles.

Flush with this fresh energy
they glow and vibrate,
displaying shimmering images
of the recently deceased that we,
in heightened awareness
during bouts of grief,
mistake for manifestations
of those we loved
and still love.

But pain subsides
and ghosts fade.
They get tired
of the constant grind
of searching for new bodies.
And then, if you want to find them,
you have to seek them out
in retirement homes, where,
haunted by old memories,
you ask them questions
they cannot answer.

Do Not Step on the Top Rung

I broke the rung barrier.
At the top of the ladder
I stepped over the apex

and just kept going.
I flashed past tree trunks.
Startled birds. Dodged a few

planes and shivered in the cold.
I watched the moon grow bigger
then recede behind me. I was

getting a workout all right,
gasping for air that wasn't
available. The stars became

worlds. The galaxy a smudge
on the black canvas behind
me. And always the future

spread out like a table cloth
inviting a place setting.
Me searching for a plate.

My Bicycle

As Avram instructed us,
my bicycle grew from a paper clip embryo,
spent some sullen time as a clothes hanger adolescent,
and has now reached its immortal phase,
a blue machine named Schwinn.

I think of its history
every time it carries me from here to there,
humming wheels and chattering gears.
And wonder if Avram ever owned a bicycle.
Wish for him, even after all these years,
the pure solace of a faithful friend.

Legends

In my imagination
the sea rises to a level
made for apocalyptic visions.
We all evolve gills and fins
just to survive,
and spend our days
straining the waters for food.
Many of us become prey to sharks
until we develop defensive strategies
involving fortified Atlantises
and the adoption of electric shock
as an effective deterrent.
When we're not hard at work
on the task of living,
we take time to tell stories
of the old days,
when we lived on land
and took oxygen from the air.
Soon a generation emerges
that regards these stories
as stupid old myths and instead
clicks what they take to be
the true tale of our species:
how we grew in the sea
and never left its benign embrace.

A Fable

Some believe when you name
a thing you create a new myth.
It is like a vaporous ghost

oozing out in a dancing ghost-
like cloud, then lodging in the name
center of our brains, where the myth

of a real world lives. It's the myth
that says a corporeal ghost
is an oddity with no name.

Name the myth, they say, to see the ghost.

The Ultimate Truth

Wouldn't it be funny
if there really was a heaven
and when you got there
they had a casino
with slot machines
and black jack tables
and everyone who ever lived
was clustered around a table
where god was at one end
shaking a pair of dice in his hand
getting mary to blow on them
then tumbling them off his palm
and all of humanity
watches those dice
roll and bounce
down the table
except for einstein
who's off in a lonely corner
halfheartedly
penciling in a keno form
and nursing a drink
muttering under his breath
saying how was he supposed to know
the way god
liked to spend his leisure time
back when the famous physicist
was appalled by the disturbing
implications of quantum theory
and came up with that phrase
about how god
does not play dice
with the universe?

Western Civilization

When Death comes calling for me
I'll kick its ass. If it tries to wrap
its bony fingers around my
prostate, I'll yank off its judge's
robe and boot it in the crotch
and laugh at its neutered empty
pelvis. If it tries planting a tumor
in my brain, I'll take that scythe
out of its hand, pull back that
hood and swing that curved
blade right through its exposed
bony neck. And then I'll stomp
on its rolling skull, crumbling
it to dust. Yeah, if Death, that
bony bastard, takes a ride in my
passenger seat with its pocket
watch swinging on the end of
a chain and tries to get me to fall
asleep at the wheel, I'll jerk my
elbow hard and fast right into
its jaw and rib cage and I'll enjoy
the sound of its splintering bones.
I'll write a death poem about my
encounter and slip it into a get
well card and send it to Death,
who will be recuperating in
some death hospital somewhere,
putting off my harvest for several
decades at least. Then I'll e-mail all
my friends about how I kicked
death's ass and they probably
won't believe me, but it won't
matter because I'll know.
I'll know death and me, we danced
to my music, at least that one time.

Some Kind of Joke

Did you hear the one
about the deity
who created these creatures
who really got out of hand
feeding fighting and fucking
in all kinds of ways
until this deity
got really pissed off
and tried wiping them out
but they just came back
stronger and more obnoxious
than they had been before
which put this deity
completely at his wit's end
so he tried walking away
from his creations
but they cried for him
in as pitiful a display
as you can imagine
and so this deity
begins feeling sorry for them
and comes back
and tries to set them
on the straight and narrow again
only it's all a trick
and these creatures wait
until the deity gets real close
and then they grab his ears
and give them a good yank
while at the same time
they punch him in the nose
pull down his pants
and spray his shorts
with a cold stream of water
until the deity
says the hell with all of you
and the creatures just laugh
and laugh and laugh
have you heard that one
have you
it's a good story
a real knee slapper.

What People Care About

Once upon a time
some sharp prodigies,
third graders
who had been
brainstorming ideas
about cosmology,
proved conclusively
that the sky
really is a dark cloth
tented over the Earth
with millions of holes
and light shining through
to give it that familiar
star twinkle we all like.
They held a press conference
to announce their findings.
Only one reporter
was there and she
asked questions
about how their
parents coped with such
smarty pants in the house.
The third graders said
you don't understand.
This is a significant finding.
The star blanket is only
about a hundred miles
away. But the reporter
shrugged and left
after a few minutes.
Then the third graders
figured out how to
build a ship to go
to the star blanket and
they stayed for a few
years sending messages
to Earth by covering up
the star holes in Morse code.
But no one noticed
so they returned to Earth

and opened up an art gallery
in New Mexico
featuring only
their own paintings.
They've been there
for many years
and if you ask them,
they'll be happy
to tell you
about the time
they overturned
accepted theories
of the universe.
Then they'll paint you
into one of their pictures
for only twenty dollars extra.

The Wake

The corpse behaved itself
for the most part.

We toasted its full past,
lamented its dismal future,

and asked the Earth
to accept it with honor.

All the while it was
as still as a painting.

We felt the stirrings
under our feet, rumbles

of hunger from the ground,
and stomped our shoes

smartly to silence
the rude anticipation.

Before we knew it,
we were all dancing.

What was left of our
friend rocked a little

with each of our steps.
This was mildly spooky.

The singing came much
later. Then the crying.

Galapagos

He said my very best friends
are the ones I can talk to
every 6 months or so. I need
my solitude but it is ok
if they come over to my island
every now and then to see
how the turtles are doing.

He had many unfinished pictures
all over the house. Some just
started, others almost complete.
These paintings will be here
after I'm dust he said. I like
that my friends want to see
how they are evolving. Actually
it helps to come intermittently.
If you see them everyday you
can't tell how much they change.

My ship was anchored at his
driveway and I sensed it was
time to board it and sail away.
Island turtles live a hundred
years, he said. Did you know
that? He dipped a brush into
paint and moved the tip close
to a canvas. I heard water
lapping at the volcanic rock
shore supporting his house.

A warm equatorial breeze ruffled
my hair as I stepped off the
island and waded through the
shallow water to my vessel.
In the rear view mirror a small
square of yellow light marked
a tiny window into the island
home of my friend the artist.
It shrunk to a pinpoint then
disappeared behind a high wave.

While Considering the Possibility of Using the Columbia River Gorge as the Setting for an Epic Fantasy

No encounter is ordinary:

The kids with their boom box cars,
thumping beat invading your gut,
become fat slugs crawling around
in the garbage. They eat anything
and leave a slimy trail that leads
to the dark places local folk avoid.

The petrographs as old as original thoughts,
hugging cooled magma like leathered skin,
inspire thoughts of divine beings
leaving messages on cliffs for the people
who listen and know there is wisdom
in the hard shell of this rock-lined scar.

Stonehenge in the darkest hour of the night,
the pillars arrayed around me like floating
buoys, prompt the creation of a giant who lived
centuries ago and in her youth played with
these blocks and left them when she grew up
and returned to the river, a mermaid crone.

Multnomah Falls looks like the draining
tears of Bigfoot crying for lost worlds.
Rock cliffs reddened by evening sunlight
transform into blood draining from wounds.
Full moon rising late over the river,
sending cool magic, healing old hurts.

Origami Landscape

The simplest elements of nature:
horizon line creasing a stretch
of blue sky over green field.

You put your hand out,
push at the fold
so the expanses collapse,
blending into a single
bluish-green sheet
that you use to make a crane
that pushes air in a current,
lifting itself on sharp folds
to a paper sun.

Out of the Park

I'm in the nose bleed seats
above the bleachers
way behind center field.

The bard swings his bat
across home plate
like a cockroach
waving his antennae.

And I'm just a fan
hoping to snag
a home run ball.

The bard lunges at all
the lousy pitches.
I groan and retreat to my
hot dog and popcorn.
Try to drink the swill
they call beer.

On the ninth pitch,
after endless foul tips,
the bard connects.
Bat cracks and the ball rises
to the clouds.
It sings above my head.
I rise with it,
drop the beer and the dog,
popcorn explodes
to the floor.

I hear the words of the bard.
A line of his epic
unravels from the ball,
floats down to my ears.

And lives there.
Missing its cork core home
bouncing now
in the parking lot behind me.

The bard is rounding third
and flying home
on quiet wings.

My Encounter With the Oracle

Before I could ask a single question
she held up her hand and took
me across the mountain to a cave.
Go to the end of this cave, she said.
All the answers you seek will be there.
Then she walked quickly away and
I entered the cave. It was wet
and cold and so narrow I had
to crawl on my belly for much
of the way. When I got to the last
wall, and could go no further,
I found a piece of thread brushing
against my face. I called the
oracle's name. She did not hear me.
I pulled the string. It
would not budge until I gave it
a good hard yank and then I
felt my heart stop. The world fractured
and a great fissure opened up beneath
me. It was so full of light I closed my eyes
as tightly as possible. But still the
radiance leaked through and traced
pictures on my retina like rock paintings.
I marveled at their primal beauty
and thanked the oracle for her strange
gift, and remained in the cave for many
years until I grew old and wary of answers.
The oracle returned then, and hit me
on the head with her hand. Are you
still here? she said.
Get out of the way now. Go home
and tend to your garden. Feed a bird.
Eat a simple meal. Sleep for several days.

After Dreams Have Scattered

After dreams have scattered
my selves to the currents
I wake and consider collecting
the soft apparitions floating.

There is the boy, still small.
Beside him the young man,
moving like nothing will hold him.

We exist beyond the cohesive powers
of epidermis and a finely honed
Western sense of independence.

If I'm not careful
I'll leave some of me behind
like a forgotten piece of clothing
that used to keep me warm
but now only makes me think
of frayed cuffs and faded colors.

Maybe I won't bother going back for it.
Just wish it well and send it
like a balloon climbing to a blue sky.

Fair Use

When the rocks passed away
the world held a long wake.

Everyone drank more than
they were used to and some

of the mourners popped open
bottles that had been stored

for centuries. We observed
the rocks still circling

our tired sky. Comets gave
us the cold shoulder. The

government began a program
to attract asteroid impacts.

Jason and the Argonauts

I remember something about golden fleece
and a sea voyage on a boat painted Technicolor green.
But none of that matters.
Decades later it's the dirty white bones
of that incredible skeleton fight
that still claws at my memory.
Ray Harryhausen spent months
on those few minutes of film,
making the bones of the dead
leap out of their graves,
arm themselves with swords, and fight.
Ray did the whole sequence in stop motion.
He exposed a frame of film,
then moved the skeleton models
a tiny fraction of an inch
then exposed another frame.
It takes twenty four frames
to make one second of screen time.
There must have been many days
when all he had to show for hours of labor
was a second or two of action. Maybe less.
In the finished movie the skeletons
wear menace and power like a suit of flesh.
I told other kids about this scene.
They mostly shrugged.
It didn't look that real to me, one of them said.
Real? But they're skeletons! Fighting skeletons!
They looked at me like my face had fallen off.
I learned to keep my mouth shut about this movie.
When it came on television
I'd watch the whole thing just for that one scene.
Those skeletons fought more fiercely than any
make believe soldier in any war movie.
They wielded their weapons from the edges of cliffs
and splashed into the ocean waiting far below
when they were beaten. They were afraid of nothing.
They broke into pieces and they crumbled back into dust,
but those skeletons swung for the stars. They lived.
For five awesome minutes Ray had given them all
a kind of glorious and awful taste of some bigger life.

The Camouflage of Fantasy

from the Bridge of the Gods
with its see-through deck
of airy steel plating quilted with
holes miraculously supporting us

and our car we see a stopped train
great snorting dragon
molded to the curves
of Columbia's flowing shore

waiting for the completion
of our passage from
Oregon to Washington
whence its secret life

of fire breath and box car scales
will resume in a resurrection
of diesel will and shrieking steel
rolling over magical track

He's the Same Age as I Am

He wears my shadow
like the wrinkled rind
wrapping an orange.

If he contains muscle or blood
or great coils of entrails,
these are secrets hidden from me.

He comes alive
at odd moments:
when the sun illuminates

the cloud of my breath
and an icicle clinging to
tree bark mimics the flow of sap.

Then a distant twist of light
invokes a double life,
and his rising form beside me

borrows my essence
for a brief sojourn, unchained
and vivid as a wing's edge.

Never the Moon

She visited the house
the other day, so full and bright
we had to wear sunglasses.

Maybe you should call them
moonglasses, she joked,
and we laughed with her.

I still have itches from
where those space ships
landed on me, she said.

We nodded. We knew the moon
had been an object of study.
And of arrogant desecration.

We apologized for the acts of
previous generations, their
mindless scratching at her skin.

She shook herself like a
trembling leaf. Don't worry
about it. These things happen.

I am something, though, aren't I?
Hanging in the sky like I do.
Who wouldn't want to reach up

and touch me? We took this
as an invitation and placed
our open palms on her silver face.

She was warm and rough
like heaps of bleached sand.
Her sighs filled the house.

As she went from full to crescent
to new we removed our glasses but she
was so dark we could not find her.

One of us said she had never been there.
I slapped my hands together
shaking moon dust to the floor.

We tracked it through the house
for the next month until it disappeared
into our porous soles.

Strange Things Can Happen on the Path Next to Falls Creek

A walk in the woods
exchanges white for green:
calcium accretions softened
to chlorophyll constructs.
My backbone becomes a stem
supporting the petal lobes
of a skull-white trillium.
My ribs flatten to a
spruce's rows of needles
and the shoulder blades
on my back become the leaves
from a giant poplar tree.
The bones of my feet
crawl into the Earth
like thick dark roots
reaching for a depth
of feeling in the cold
dirt. My femur wants
to be a tree supporting
the sky. And my kneecap
seeks the rush of life
associated with the tight urge
straining in the simplest
bud of spring bursting
to a quiet sculpted perfection.

Mark

The giant
strides out of
the canyon where they live
and tells me she
wants a tattoo
of her sweetheart's name
on her shoulder.
She stretches out on the grass
while I assemble
my equipment:
ladder
needles
ink pots
pump
rags
and straw hat for my head.
I have needled many giants before,
their vast skin
a living canvas
for kitsch and high art,
and now I charge by the gallon.
I put up the ladder,
caution the giant to
please be still,
and climb to the top rung,
my hoses slung over my shoulder.
As I set to work
I ask if the giant felt the
earthquake last night
that rattled my walls
and shook my bed
but the giant says nothing:
they are not given to
small talk
and silently
I push needles into her skin.
Inject ink.
Wipe away excess.
It is hard work
and I need an

assistant
but tattooing is a fading
business in our village.
No young person wants
to apprentice to me
so I am perched precariously
on this ladder
alone
hoping the giant does not
twitch or shake
her arm.
I make the letter M.
It takes a long while
and when I finish and
begin on A
the giant
starts leaking tears.
They fall to the grass
where I hear them
before seeing them.
I pause and lick
my lips and look at the
giant who avoids my
eyes. I am an
insect
biting her arm.
What is it? I ask.
Is the needle too painful?
She closes her eyes and
shakes her head
and I finish the second
letter,
begin on the R
and finally she speaks,
her breath rushing into
the air like a hot
wind.
He died last night
she says.
Jumped off

the canyon edge
and lies crumpled
at the bottom
right now.
My hand stops for an instant
then continues.
The sun is hot today
and I am weary
but I finish
the R
and move onto the
K
and after what
seems a long time I
finish
the name of the giant
who disturbed my
sleep last night.
The new bearer of his
name remains on the
ground outside my
house for the rest of the
day mourning her
loss while I try twice
to hold her hand.

Dramatis Personae

alien • 38
ancestors • 44
angels • 30, 44
ant • 24
apparitions • 13
artist • 83
arugula • 25
Atlas • 45
authorities • 20
Barbie • 32
bard • 86
beach • 25
Bigfoot • 38, 84
birds • 29, 34, 73
blind woman • 23
body • 17, 40
bodyguards • 32
books • 41
bugs • 29, 63
Captain Supremo • 20
cat • 53, 66
characters • 39
cheese • 25
children • 11, 18, 23, 50, 54, 56, 61, 80, 91
clocks • 27, 35, 53
clouds • 49
coins • 67
colony • 24
companions • 21
congressional committee • 32
contractors • 12
corpse • 72, 82
county commissioner • 38
cows • 23
creatures • 16, 34, 79
criminals • 20
cumin • 25
Davidson, Avram • 74
Death • 14, 78
death • 66
deity • 79
dental floss • 25
Doc • 17
dog • 23
doll house • 23, 28
dove • 67
dragon • 92
Earth • 28, 35, 45, 69, 71, 80, 82, 96
editors • 20
Einstein, Albert • 77
entrepreneur • 54
fairies • 12, 56
family • 47
fans • 20, 32, 86
flowchart • 25
flowers • 67
friends • 14, 46, 74, 78, 82, 83
gas station attendant • 23
Ghost • 66
ghost • 13, 22, 40, 44, 62, 66, 70, 72, 76
giants • 58, 84, 97
god • 77
greeters • 44
Harryhausen, Ray • 91
he • 26, 40, 55
heras • 36
heroes • 36
Jason • 91
keeper • 11

kelp • 25, 71
Ken • 33
keys • 48
kids • 43, 84, 91
librarians • 39, 64
luna moth • 25
magician • 67
man • 52, 69
Mark • 97
Mary • 77
materialists • 13
me • 11, 12, 14, 23, 24, 27, 28, 29, 31, 34, 43, 44, 49, 53, 54, 57, 58, 60, 61, 63, 64, 67, 70, 71, 73, 75, 83, 86, 88, 89, 93, 96
moon • 54, 62, 69, 84, 94
mountain • 23, 26
mourners • 90
Nietzsche, Friedrich • 43
nurse • 17
officer • 39
old man • 36
oracle • 88
parents • 21, 80
patient • 17
Pegasus • 28
people • 11, 16, 17, 19, 36, 41, 50, 64, 65, 84
pig • 59
pixies • 65
poets • 54
protagonists • 39
quilt maker • 14
rabbit • 67
rainbow • 25
rational types • 17

raven-haired beauty • 14
reporter • 80
rock • 90
sea • 71, 75
shadow • 93
shark • 75
she • 62
shopkeeper • 31
Shuster, Joe • 43
Siegel, Jerry • 43
skeletons • 91
slug • 52, 84
soul • 50, 61
spider • 23
spouse • 50
Stick Man • 20
stones • 42
sunspots • 25
Superman • 43
Supreme Fascist • 16
surgeon • 17
tattooist • 97
telephones • 14, 19
tongue • 25
truck • 25
villains • 39
we • 18, 19, 21, 35, 75, 82, 94
wedding guests • 68
weeping willow • 29
wise man • 22
wolf • 59
words • 30, 62
worms • 63
you • 13, 19, 22, 30, 44, 46, 50, 52, 64, 65, 70, 71, 72, 77, 79, 81, 85

101

Acknowledgements

The poems in *Fantasy Life* are previously unpublished, except as noted here:

"Doll, Still Living" originally appeared in *Margie*, Volume 2, 2004.

"A Field Guide to the Phosphenes" originally appeared in *Full Unit Hookup*, #2, Summer 2002.

"The Great Divide" originally appeared in *Asimov's SF*, April 2002.

"Lunar Fate" originally appeared in *Lady Churchill's Rosebud Wristlet*, #13, November 2003.

"Mark" originally appeared in *Dreams and Nightmares*, #59, May 2001.

"My Bicycle" originally appeared in *Asimov's SF*, August 2004.

"Super Hero Takes the Month Off" originally appeared in *Wavelength*, #8, Winter 2003-2004.

"Time's Apologist" originally appeared in *Into the Teeth of the Wind*, Volume 3, Issue 3, 2003.

"Twelve Things a Man Should Do After Dying" originally appeared in *Nuthouse*, #7, Spring 2003.

"The Ultimate Truth" originally appeared in *Into the Teeth of the Wind*, Volume IV, issue 2-4, 2004.

"The Unexpected Unexplained" originally appeared in *Asimov's SF*, October/November 2002.

"Unlikely to Happen Any Time Soon" originally appeared in *Asimov's SF*, January 2004.

"We Are All Ghosts" originally appeared in *The Magazine of Speculative Poetry*, Volume 6, #3, Spring 2004.

"When I Die" originally appeared in *Snake Nation Review*, #16, 2003.

"While Considering the Possibility of Using the Columbia River Gorge as the Setting for an Epic Fantasy" originally appeared in *Mythic Delirium*, #9, Summer/Fall 2003.

"Wondering What They Are Up to in the Middle of the Night" originally appeared in *Asimov's SF*, May 2002.

"The World is a Strange Place" originally appeared in *Confluence*, Volume 13, 2002.

About the Author

Mario Milosevic lives with his wife, novelist Kim Antieau, in Bigfoot country in Washington State on the banks of the Columbia River, where he works at a small town library. His poems have appeared in many print and online journals, and in the anthology *Poets Against the War*. A companion volume, *Animal Life*, is also available.

www.ingramcontent.com/pod-product-compliance
Lightning Source LLC
Chambersburg PA
CBHW020144130526
44591CB00030B/211